UNSTUCK:

8 STEPS YOU CAN TAKE

Right Now To Possess
Your Promise

Felicia Howell LaBoy

ACKNOWLEDGMENTS

No work is ever created in isolation. Everyone has a tribe of folks who love, support, encourage and challenge them to be greater than they think they are. I am especially and eternally grateful to:

God – for the inspiration of for this book and for His love and saving grace.

Adrian LaBoy, my husband – for the love, support and encouragement to always follow my dreams. You are indeed God's perfect match for me.

SanDawna Ashley and Ramona Payne – for the gift of sisterhood, love, friendship and always insisting on more and greater for me.

Cynthia Peer and Rhonda Petit – for your friendship and encouragement to pursue and complete this book.

Darlene Martin – for your friendship, encouragement, investment and creativity that always insists I shine.

Shirley Francis Manigault, my aunt and role model – for your support, encouragement and love. I am where I am because you have modeled a clear path for me and reached back to help me along the way.

Every time you cross my mind, I break out in exclamations of thanks to God. Each exclamation is a trigger to prayer. I find myself praying for you with a glad heart.

Philippians 1:3 – 4, The Message Bible

DEDICATION

For my sister Rosalinde Franchette Howell and my brother Harold Francis Howell who have always insisted that with God's help, I am well able to become, have or do anything I desire.

TABLE OF CONTENTS

INTRODUCTION

I know what it's like — to make the same resolutions every January of every year, only to see your enthusiasm and resolve fizzle out before March 1st. Like me, you may have even told yourself that this is the year – the year you will move towards your dreams. You pray. You make plans and set goals. Then it happens — an opportunity opens to finally do that thing you have always wanted. All your friends and family believe you've got what it takes and say they are behind you 100%. and what happens? You choke. Something, anything, comes up to tell you that you aren't ready or are not good enough. So, the opportunity passes by and you think — "Well, God must not have meant that for me."

> *Failure is simply the opportunity to begin again, this time more intelligently.*
>
> **Henry Ford**

Worse yet, when we've been bold enough to take the "leap" and move towards our dream, our promise, we find out that there is much more involved than we thought. So, although we start moving towards our promise, the dreams in our heart that won't go away, we still find ourselves derailed. We sabotage ourselves. We procrastinate. We quit after a few tries or when we have a misstep. We falsely believe that opposition and struggle are simply signs that this is "not our season" for accomplishing our dreams and fulfilling our destiny.

Hope deferred makes the heart sick, but a longing fulfilled is a tree of life.

Proverbs 13:20

So, we turn back with broken hearts silently wondering what is so wrong with us that we cannot have the desire of our hearts. Worse still, we believe the lies of the enemy that somehow, we are not worthy of all the blessings that God wants to bestow on us.

What if you changed your perspective and saw what you're facing as a sign that you're exactly where God wants you to be, because giants are the welcome committee in the Promised Land?

Steven Furtick

After a while, we simply just stop trying because we believe one of a few things. First, we think "it's too late; we missed our opportunity." Second, we think "we're too old to learn or be anything different." Third, we believe that securing our promise won't require courage or some very hard work. Fourth and finally, although we've put in a tremendous amount of work and have a lot of experience, somehow deep down we either believe we don't deserve it or that we are not good enough and/or do not have enough time, intelligence, money, etc. to secure our dreams or maintain them.

Remember your dreams and fight for them. You must know what you want from life. There is just one thing that makes your dream become impossible: the fear of failure

Paulo Coelho

Beloved, if any of these sounds like you, you are in good company. The feelings of not being good enough or not having enough are fear-based. In fact, most people in the world struggle with insecurity and fear. Often this is why the first words God gives someone that He has marked for an awesome task is "Fear (or Fret) not." Note that God is not saying, "Don't feel the fear." Rather He is offering encouragement and the support to begin by reminding us to just acknowledge that the fear and insecurity are there, but so is God.

Rather than believing the promises of God or that God loves them and will help them accomplish more than they ever thought they could in their own strength, many people settle for an "okay" life. They believe they should be thankful for what they have because they are better off than most -- so, why should they complain? All the while they yearn for something greater than they are currently experiencing. They know deep down inside that they were created for more. Worse still, they do not understand that the very desire in their hearts that won't go away is an indication that God is calling them higher. So, they remain "stuck" – blessed but not challenged or fulfilled.

For the few brave souls willing to at least consider their dreams, there are thousands of self-help books, seminars, webinars, You-Tube videos, podcasts, CDs, DVDs, etc. to provide anyone with the steps they need to take to achieve the life, any life they want. Although this information is quite useful and beneficial, many of us do not know how this fits with who we are as people of faith, especially Christians, whose greatest desire is to live in the will of God and to fulfill His purpose for our lives.

Simply put, many of us feel we don't need a self-help book to tell us how to live. We believe that the Spirit of God and the Word of God are sufficient to help us over any hurdle. So, we read our Bibles and still find ourselves, stuck – setting resolutions, believing for "breakthroughs" and "harvests" that seem out of reach.

"To whom much is given, much is required" is not as much about the trial we must endure. Rather, it is a statement about how God intends for us to use the talents and abilities we've been given. To not utilize our gifts to their full capacity is to sin against God.

Anonymous

If this sounds like you, I invite you to join me in turning to the Bible for help in making good on our goals and resolutions, what the Bible refers to as our "promise," and see if we can glean some important steps to help us co-create with God the life that God intends for us. To help us along the journey, I propose that we look at someone who was blessed but knew what it was like to walk around in circles for a long time – never achieving what was promised. Someone who, after 40 years of waiting and as a senior citizen, finally accomplished the dream that God put in his heart.

*You are never too old to set another goal or to dream
a new dream.*

C.S. Lewis

Who am I talking about? Why, Joshua, of course. You know who I mean. Joshua, son of Nun, Moses' assistant, and the second leader of the nation of Israel. Joshua, who as a man, one could argue a man well past his prime, finally accomplished the goal and dream God had placed in his heart some 40 years earlier.

Whereas, we could literally spend a lifetime studying this remarkable man of God, I want to suggest that there are 8 simple steps that Joshua took that can provide you and I with a strategy to begin to walk in the life that all our goals and resolutions are meant to achieve -- the life that God has purposed for us.

Better yet, all these steps are found in God's commissioning of Joshua in Joshua 1: 1 – 9. In fact, it can be argued that the remainder of the book of Joshua is simply Joshua going back to God's original call for him as found in this passage, and repeating these steps over and over until he had accomplished his dream of dwelling in the Promised Land. Therefore, although each step towards our success will come from one or more of the verses in Joshua 1: 1 – 9, this devotional will highlight passages of Scripture from various parts of the Bible to show you how Joshua put these steps into practice as a model for you.

Because I know your faith is important to you, I have organized these 8 steps as something you can use in your quiet time in place of your regular devotion. To move you beyond simply reading to action, each step is accompanied by Key Memory Verse(s), a devotional, a prayer starter and a place for you to journal about six things:

1. What is God saying to you through the Key Memory Verse(s) and the devotional?

2. How can you implement this step and move one step closer to your goal/resolution/promise?

3. What may hinder you in taking this step and how will you get around it?

4. How will you celebrate/acknowledge when you've taken this step (i.e., post on FB)?

5. If you didn't do the step, why or why not?

6. Identify what you need to address to accomplish this step.

While I'll give you some place to capture your answers to these questions briefly in each devotional, I suggest that you purchase a separate notebook or journal to record your answers and as a memorial for you to look back on when you've "possessed your promise."

Finally, beloved, because neither Rome, Canaan, nor even your promise will happen in a day; this process asks you to "take possession of your promise" one day, one reasonable step at a time. Building on the best productivity research available, I invite you to use this process for no more than 7 – 10 goals that you wish to accomplish in a year that are part of the larger "promise" you wish to possess (i.e., the fullness of the vision for your entire life, not just one aspect of it). Out of that list, choose no more than 2 – 3 goals that you wish to achieve per quarter, rather than trying to tackle everything all at once. Then break these quarterly goals into smaller ones that stretch, but not overwhelm you. If you do this you will, like Joshua, eventually devise a strategy for each goal that helps you move towards you promise one reasonable step at a time. Over a year's time, you will be amazed at just how far you've traveled just going one step at a time.

Just in case you're wondering, experts say that it took Joshua 7 years of imperfect progress to conquer the Promised Land!

> *It is better to take many small steps in the right direction than to make a great leap forward only to stumble backward.*
>
> **Anonymous**

Simply put, no matter what it is that you want to achieve, this process is designed to help you acknowledge the dream God has placed in your heart and to get unstuck, so that you can be in position to succeed in bringing it to pass. More importantly, it is designed to help you tackle your dreams one simple step at a time so that you are always moving forward.

I don't care how long it's been. I don't care if you think you're too old. If you are willing to be and do something different, your latter days can be much better than your former ones. Besides, you are probably the one that your family, your friends and your community have been waiting for. So why don't you stir up your faith, tell your fears to be quiet and move towards your dreams? Remember, that nothing God ordains will be impossible if you rely on His presence and instruction.

Don't believe me – just ask Joshua!

Our deepest fear is not that we are inadequate. Our deepest fear is that we are powerful beyond measure. It is our light, not our darkness that most frightens us. We ask ourselves, "Who am I to be brilliant, gorgeous, talented, fabulous?"

Actually, who are you not to be? You are a child of God. Your playing small does not serve the world. There is nothing enlightened about shrinking so that other people won't feel insecure around you.

We are all meant to shine, as children do. We were born to make manifest the glory of God that is within us. It's not just in some of us; it's in everyone. And as we let our own light shine, we unconsciously give other people permission to do the same.

As we are liberated from our own fear, our presence automatically liberates others.

Marianne Williamson

STEP 1

Acknowledge What's Dead, Bury It and Move On.

SOMETHING GREATER IS WAITING FOR YOU IF YOU WILL NOT TRY TO BRING YOUR PAST INTO YOUR FUTURE.

DAILY BIBLE READING:

Joshua 1: 1 – 9

KEY MEMORY VERSE(S):

[1] After the death of Moses the servant of the Lord, the Lord said to Joshua son of Nun, Moses' aide:

[2a] "Moses my servant is dead. Now then…

(Joshua 1:1 – 2a, NIV)

DEVOTIONAL:

We must be willing to let go of the life we've planned, so as to have the life that is waiting for us.

Joseph Campbell

One of the main reasons many of us are stuck and stay stuck is because we have a hard time identifying what is dead and should be buried in our lives. Simply put, we have a hard time letting go of what once worked for us. We hold onto dead relationships, dead-end jobs and dead images of ourselves – who we were and who we are based on someone else's definition. Moreover, we hold onto stuff that keeps us "living with the dead" and holding onto a past that is crippling us now and that is killing off our dreams.

Let me ask some questions so you can know what I mean. How many of us are still trying to live up to a parent's ideal of who and what we should be? How many of us are still trying to be who we once were, not acknowledging how time and experience has made us better (Don't act like you don't know what I mean – some stuff we did, (and wore) at 25 definitely isn't "cute" at 55)? How many of us are doing some things we know we have outgrown, because we don't have a full appreciation of ourselves – our own opinions and values?

> *Life goes on whether you choose to move on and take a chance in the unknown or stay behind, locked in the past, thinking of what could have been.*
>
> **Stephanie Smith**

For the majority of Joshua's adult life, Moses has been there – leading him, guiding him, supporting him. Every major victory in Joshua's life can be attributed in no small way to Joshua's connection to Moses. He was freed from slavery because of Moses; conquered the Amalekites because of Moses (Exodus 17: 8 – 13); experienced the Promised Land and tasted the grapes of Canaan because of Moses (Numbers 13 – 14); received the Law of God (the Ten Commandments and the other rules for living according to God's ways) because of Moses; and developed a deep and abiding relationship with God by meeting in the Tent of Meeting just like Moses (Exodus 33: 7 – 11). To say that Moses is one of the most influential, if not the most influential person in Joshua's life, is no understatement.

And yet in this passage from Joshua 1: 1-9, the very first thing God says to Joshua is "Moses, my servant is dead." Duh? If anyone knows that Moses is dead, it's Joshua. So, we must ask ourselves, why did God feel it necessary to say this to Joshua? I think it is because God wants Joshua to know that He's done with Moses and intends to use Joshua. How do we know this? Because in verse 5, God promises to be with Joshua, like God was with Moses.

Simply put, by reminding Joshua that Moses is dead and by promising that God will be with him, God is saying to Joshua, "Now, it's your turn – your turn to spread your wings; your turn to move from being behind the scenes to taking center stage; your turn to lead the people based on what you know. Remember of the Israelites only Joshua and Caleb know what Canaan is like – both its opportunities and its challenges.

God's not looking for a poor facsimile of Moses, God wants to use Joshua – his gifts, his graces (ways of being and doing) and his experience – not Moses'. If Joshua doesn't understand that the time of "Moses" is over, he will never use his own "stuff" – his experience as a military strategist, his knowledge of Canaan and his relationship and submission to God to lead Israel in conquering Canaan.

So, what about you and me? Have we taken the time to examine what we are currently doing that should have been buried long ago? Are we still responding to others because they remind us of the person who left us, the person who abandoned us or even persons who loved us that we are still trying to answer? Are we still trying to prove to someone who is dead and gone that we matter and that our choices are okay? Are we still trying to make up for a "mistake" that we made in our youth rather than forgiving ourselves and moving on?

Beloved, your "Moses" and my "Moses" is dead, and we need to bury him/it and get on with the thing that is in our hearts to do. But first, to bury "Moses," we've got to identify him/it. We've got to identify what's "dead" and not working, determine if it can or should be revived, and if it is truly dead, bury it and move on.

Sometimes you have to let things go so there's room for better things to come into your life.

Adrian Body

I don't know about you, but I have some dreams and desires that I want to achieve before I leave the planet. But to do so, I (and you) need to go on a hunt – a hunt to figure out what is dead, so we can bury it, grieve it and move on.

Today is a great day for a funeral – to say "goodbye" to something that if you don't bury it, will bury you. Be warned it will hurt. Anything that meant something to you must be grieved. Then say "Good bye, thank you for helping me be who I am." Then let it go – don't dig it up anymore.

Forget what hurt you in the past, but never forget what it taught you. However, if it taught you to hold onto grudges, seek revenge, not forgive or show compassion, to categorize people as good or bad, to distrust and be guarded with your feelings then you didn't learn a thing. God doesn't bring you lessons to close your heart. He brings you lessons to open it...

Shannon L. Adler

PRAYER STARTER:

Lord, thank you that you are a God who keeps your promises. Thank you for the restlessness in my heart that lets me know that you have more in store for me. Please let me know what in my life you are finished with. Help me to grieve it, rid myself of anything associated with it, and let it go. Amen.

JOURNAL QUESTIONS:

1) What is God saying to you through the Bible verse and the devotional?

2) How can you implement this step and move one step closer to your goal/resolution/promise?

3) What may hinder you in taking this step and how will you get around it?

4) How will you celebrate/acknowledge when you've taken this step (i.e., post on Facebook; share with a friend)?

5) If you didn't do this step, why or why not?

6) Identify what you need to address or resolve to accomplish this step, the support you may need, and when you'll begin addressing this.

STEP 2

Get Ready To Possess Your Promise (Dream).

SUCCESS CAN BE YOURS IF YOU PREPARE AND WORK HARD.

DAILY BIBLE READING:

Joshua 1:10 – 15

KEY MEMORY VERSE(S):

² "Moses my servant is dead. Now then, you and all these people, get ready to cross the Jordan River into the land I am about to give to them—to the Israelites.

(Joshua 1:2 NIV)

DEVOTIONAL:

It amazes me how much people who say they feel called to, or even want to do something, never take the first step in realizing their dreams. I still remember attending a Christian conference early on in my walk with God that showed me the power of taking at least one step toward your dreams. I was attending a workshop on being a missionary – not because I wanted to be a missionary, it was just the only workshop I could get into.

Anyway, the missionary leading the workshop asked two key questions. First, "who wants to be or feels called to be involved in worldwide missions?" Every hand shot up, except mine. Then she asked, "how many of you have a passport?" and only my hand was raised. Here I was in a room of people who were certain that God had called them to do worldwide missions and not one of them had a passport, save the person(me) who was "sure "God HAD NOT called them to worldwide missions. Even more alarming was that most of these persons had not even investigated to see what it took to get one.

> *Take the first step in faith. You don't have to see the whole staircase, just take the first step.*
>
> **Martin Luther King, Jr.**

While it can be very easy to judge people who do not take the first step toward something that we have already conquered or accomplished, I submit to you, that all us have an area in our lives in which we have failed to get ready for action. From something as simple as buying a new pair of sneakers to begin an exercise program or contacting a few schools to see what is required to finally get that degree or to reviewing our schedule to see what we need to stop doing or delegate. These are the first steps to finally do what we want and need to do to move forward and improve our lives and the lives of those around us.

> *The first step to living the life you want is leaving the life you don't want. Taking the first step forward is always the hardest. But then each step forward gets easier and easier. And each step forward gets you closer and closer until eventually what had once been invisible starts to be visible. And what had once felt impossible starts to feel possible.*
>
> **Karen Salmansohn**

Simply put, we fail to get ready by taking the very first, and often small step to move towards the actions needed to possess our promise. Beloved, we need to get ready by doing something – not pray on it, not wait for God to move.

From our reading today, we know that immediately after hearing God's commission to lead the people to possess the Promised Land (Joshua 1: 1 – 9), Joshua starts getting himself and the people ready. He does this by ordering the officials to "go through the camp and tell the people, 'Get your provisions ready. Three days from now you will cross the Jordan here to go in and take possession of the land the Lord your God is giving you for your own.'" *(Joshua 1:10-11).*

See Beloved, the simple fact is that God will not begin to work with us to possess our promise until we take the first step to get ready. Too many of us are waiting on God, when in fact God is waiting on us.

Getting ready by taking even a small initial step is an act of faith. It means that we believe the promise God has made us. It is putting our "mustard seed" amount of faith to work by saying to ourselves, "I don't know how it is going to happen, but because God said so, I'm going to get ready."

You can pray until you faint, but unless you get up and try to do something, God is not going to put it in your lap.

Fannie Lou Hamer

Go ahead; get ready; bust a move. Take that first step. Acknowledge the fear and just do it (afraid) anyhow knowing that God is with you and for you to help you succeed (Isaiah 41:8-10).

Why?

Because you've got nothing to lose, especially when you put your faith in God and not in yourself alone.

Because great things are possible when you and I believe and act on, not just "claim" the promises of God (Matthew 17: 20 – 21).

> *Much of your experience and success or failure or fulfillment or faithfulness in life, depends on you. Of course, apart from the grace of God we can do nothing, but God seems to respect us too much to do everything for us without our effort and involvement.*
>
> **Jeremy Rivera**

PRAYER STARTER:

Lord, I admit I am a procrastinator. Even though I say I want things to change, I am really afraid that I will not be up to the task. If I'm honest, I am better at talking about my goals than actually achieving them. I agree with you that this should not be so. Please help me to break my habit of procrastination. Give me the faith, wisdom and courage to begin and not to be sidetracked. Thank you in advance, Amen

JOURNAL QUESTIONS:

1) What is God saying to you through the Bible verse and the devotional?

2) How can you implement this step and move one step closer to your goal/resolution/promise?

3) What may hinder you in taking this step and how will you get around it?

4) How will you celebrate/acknowledge when you've taken this step (i.e., post on Facebook; share with a friend)?

5) If you didn't do this step, why or why not?

6) Identify what you need to address or resolve to accomplish this step, the support you may need, and when you'll begin addressing this.

STEP 3

Get A Big Vision

YOU CAN ONLY HAVE THE FUTURE YOU SEE AND THAT IS WORTH STRIVING FOR.

DAILY BIBLE READING:

Numbers 13: 17 – 30 (NIV)

KEY MEMORY VERSE(S):

³ I will give you every place where you set your foot, as I promised Moses. ⁴ Your territory will extend from the desert to Lebanon, and from the great river, the Euphrates—all the Hittite country—to the Mediterranean Sea in the west.

(Joshua 1:3-4 NIV)

DEVOTIONAL:

Did you know that recent studies have found that multitasking reduces our productivity by 40%?

Yes. I said, 40% -- that's almost half.

MULTITASKING ALSO:

- Damages our brains by putting them on overload;
- Makes us dumb by destroying our ability to know what is important and what isn't;
- Makes us prone to cheat and cut corners;
- Makes us think that so-called "productivity" tools are helping us when they aren't;

- Lowers the quality of our work because we are sloppy in our execution;

- Reduces the ability to make connections between what we are learning and what we are doing and were doing; and

- Requires more of us in terms of workload (remember – it lessens our productivity by almost half.)[1]

In fact, New York Times best-selling author and productivity specialist, Michael Hyatt says that one sure way to not succeed in accomplishing our goals is to set and try to accomplish too many goals each year. To describe how unproductive going after too many things at once is, Hyatt says "Man/Woman who chases two rabbits catches neither."[2]

So why do we think that we must multitask, especially those of the household of God? I think there are three main reasons. First, we are trying to make sure that we are keeping up with everyone else's life, so we try to be excellent at all things at once without taking into consideration our life circumstances, gifts, aptitudes, or talents for doing certain things.

Second, some church leaders suggest that we ought to "wear out for God" (i.e., stay busy and overloaded) rather than "rust out (sitting around and doing nothing);" by highlighting Biblical characters as models of perfection. For example, the Proverbs 31 woman who is described as a wife, mother, excellent home-manager and entrepreneur is often highlighted as the model for ideal Christian womanhood.

---

[1] Julie Neidlinger, "The Horrifying Truth About Multitasking," CoSchedule Blog, November 19, 2014, https://coschedule.com/blog/multitasking-and-productivity/
[2] Michael Hyatt, "Navigate Your Way to Success in 2018: 5 Blunders that Could Shipwreck Your Goals (and How to Avoid Them)," [Free, Limited Webinar], December 12, 2018.

While it is true that she was all these things, nothing in the text tells us that she did *all* these things *at once*.

> *Multitasking divides your attention and leads to confusion and weakened focus.*
>
> **Deepak Chopra**

Now I am all for helping people to find their spiritual gifts and to get busy doing the work of ministry. But…. I am also sure that the Bible has an incredible amount of Scriptures that speak of the need for resting (Sabbath); of taking long seasons to rejuvenate (Jubilee) and of being still. In fact, I think it is erroneous to preach and teach that people are or should be in "harvest" season all the time. This is not the model the Bible shows us (see Ecclesiastes 3 or Genesis 22). Neither is it what we see in nature.

Although these two reasons are significant, I believe the biggest reason we multitask, get overwhelmed or worn out and give up is we don't discern ourselves the vision that God has for us. We also don't consult God regarding whether we should or shouldn't accept whatever vision, responsibilities or challenges others lay out for us. In this way, we become what others say or think we should be without learning to appreciate ourselves or follow our dreams.

We take it all on, trying to become excellent multitaskers so that we can "have favor with God and humans" (Luke 2:52). We don't only "wear out for God-" we wear out ourselves. Sometimes those closest to us too. We keep going until we burnout and get so depressed and discouraged that we just quit.

When the Bible likens ministry to sowing and reaping, it suggests God will bring His fruit in its time. Nothing good grows overnight, and the farmer must be patient.

Anonymous

When we do try to follow our dreams, as soon as we run into and obstacle or someone questions why we are doing what we do, we back down. We mistakenly believe that the trouble and the criticism are signs that we are on the wrong path.

But apparently a sign of God's will is not the ease with which you obtain it. Apparently, the very sign that you've made it to the Promised Land is giants. Conflict. Opposition.

Stephen Furtick

We make the false assumption that if we failed at something before we will fail again. Then we resolve ourselves to failure or simply plan to try again next year even though we have this nagging feeling that "this won't be our year either." Worse still and quite heartbreaking is that many of us just begin to believe that God didn't mean for us to accomplish our dreams first place.

Beloved, nothing could be further from the truth. One failure does not mean that one is doomed to failure. As someone has said, "mistakes (failure) are simply signposts that learning is going on." Sometimes the failure is meant to strengthen us. Sometimes it is meant for us to really question ourselves as to whether we are living out someone else's vision for our lives – our parents', our spouses', our kids', our employers', our churches', or our cliques. Sometimes stuff just happens.

> *Don't let others tell you what you can't do. Don't let the limitations of others limit your vision. If you can remove your self-doubt and believe in yourself, you can achieve what you never thought possible.*
>
> **Roy T. Bennett**

The problem with all of this is that by trying to live into someone else's vision for us and believing the hype about multitasking, we are spiritually, mentally, emotionally and physically walking around in circles making little to no progress toward the dreams that are in our heart. And while this may create a "blessed" surviving mode of life, it does not create the kind of blessed, passionate and thriving kind of life that God intends and that has the potential of attracting others to life in God.

To get back to our Bible reading for today and to put everything in context, the Israelites were just a short distance, an 11-day journey from having all that God had promised. And yet because they could only see themselves as others saw them, they spent 40 years wandering around in circles. Yes, God still blessed them by sending manna daily and making sure their clothes and shoes never ran out. However, this was nothing compared to how God originally intended to bless them.

If there was ever a person who knew what it meant to walk around in circles because of someone else's vision or lack thereof, it was Joshua. Although Joshua and Caleb believed that God had given the Promised Land to the Israelites, they had to walk around for 40 years not accomplishing what God had put into their hearts because of the unbelief and fear of others (Numbers 14:1-38). Furthermore, it wasn't even their fault that they spent 40 years going around in circles – it was the fault of others who went with them who could not believe the promise of God.

Beloved, let me tell you this, if you are going to possess your promise, there are three things you will have to do: Get A Big Vision; Know Your Why, and Stretch Yourself One Step At A Time. We'll talk about getting a vision in this step and then focus "knowing your why" and on stretching yourself one step at a time in the next step.

In Joshua 1: 3 – 4, God is not only clear that every place Joshua has set his foot will belong to him, but God even sets the parameters for Joshua. Also, you will notice that unlike Moses or the rest of the Israelites except Caleb, Joshua does not argue with God about the vision being too big or too challenging. He just accepts it. And he trusts that God will keep God's promise to be with him to accomplish it.

How about you? What is the dream that God has put into your heart? Is the main reason why you have not gone for it is because you think it is too big? Or perhaps you think you don't deserve it or can't attain it? Or perhaps it is because your family or current circle of friends and associates have never done or can't see how/why you should even try? Is it perhaps because your church or religious clique doesn't "believe it's God" for you to move forward? Looking out for your interests, they tell you to "play it safe," or "be reasonable." They even go so far as to tell you why you can't have the life you dream of – all to protect you of course.

God would not have put the dream in your heart, if he hadn't already given you everything you need to fulfill it.

Joel Osteen

In Deuteronomy 7, God tells the Israelites two things. First, God is clear that what God will do for them is not based on their abilities nor whether they deserve it or not (Deuteronomy 7:7-10). The fulfillment of their dreams (and ours) is based on one thing and one thing only – the love and faithfulness of God. They (and us) will succeed only by God's grace and God's mercy.

When I dare to be powerful, to use my strength in the service of my vision, then it becomes less and less important whether I am afraid.

Audre Lord

What about us? Is the reason we fail to dream big dreams or to lay hold of the secret passions of our heart is because we think we don't have the skills? Perhaps, we are too afraid to try because we don't believe that someone like us deserves what our hearts long for? We see ourselves as "grasshoppers" (small and insignificant) who are unable to conquer whatever giant (obstacle) that is keeping us from the possessing our promise (Numbers 13:32-33).

Beloved, nothing could be further from the truth. God promises that with the giving of the Holy Spirit, we will dream and have visions that are divinely inspired (Acts 2:17-21). As a matter of fact, the Bible goes so far as to say no matter how big we dare to hope, dream or think, God is able to do infinitely more (Ephesians 3:20).

If you don't need a God to pull off what you're planning, you are not dreaming big enough.

Michael Hyatt

So, before you even begin to dare to dream, let me suggest that before you start, determine that all throughout the process you will PLAY FULL OUT. Swing for the fences. Go for broke. Act as if you have nothing to fear or lose and lay out the dreams you have for your life, remembering that the Bible promises that "God has prepared things for those who love him that no eye has seen, or ear has heard, or that haven't crossed the mind of any human being" (1 Corinthians 2:9 Common English Bible).

Better yet, pray and ask God to show you the vision God had for your life when God created you. Be prepared to be amazed. Know that God never intended for you to accomplish it without him, but that with Him the impossible will be possible. Once you have gotten your vision, write it down and meditate on it until it becomes real in your heart and soul.

Also, keep in mind that you can't share the vision with everyone, because everyone can't see it. Sometimes, even if they can, they can't see it in you. Sometimes they are just jealous and envious. Don't be discouraged and don't waste time trying to convince them of what God has told you. God hasn't given them the vision/the dream. God has given it to you.

That said, you should pray about who you can share your dream/vision with. According to Proverbs 15:22 "without counsel, plans go wrong, but with many advisers they succeed." None of us knows everything. It is just plain stupid to reinvent the wheel. It is prideful not to ask for help with things you are unfamiliar with.

There are many people who would be glad to assist you in getting where you want to go. There are also many folks who are skilled in areas that you are not who for a moderate price can do some of the work that can free you to focus on what you're good at. I've found many of these folks on Fiverr and Upwork and/or by talking persons who are already doing what I desire to.

Make a conscious effort to surround yourself with positive, nourishing, and uplifting people.

Jack Canfield

Here are some examples of the assistance that you might need to get to launch your vision. If you want to go back to school, look to see if the school you want to attend has a program targeted for adult learners who have been out of school for a while and make an appointment. If you want to write a book, check out your local community college, library and even YouTube to see if there is a quick workshop or webinar that you can attend that could help you.

If you want to start that business, check out the Senior Core of Retired Executives (www.score.org) to get some mentoring from a retired executive who is just looking to help someone get started in creating and succeeding in their own business. If you want to pick up a hobby – painting, photography, etc., check out your local library, community college or community newspaper to see if there is a moderately priced class somewhere. You can also check out EventBrite or MeetUp to learn new skills, pick up a hobby and/or make friends with like-minded people.

These are some examples, but the principle is the same. If you want to do something, find out who is doing it, see where and how they are sharing their expertise and their skills, humble yourself (i.e., be willing to look "stupid"), sign up for whatever they are offering and show up for what you sign up for.

I can already hear you thinking – where will I get the money or the time?

> *God never gives you a dream that matches your budget. He's not checking your bank account. He's checking your faith.*
>
> ***Anonymous***

Beloved, remember Step 1 where we talked about identifying some things that no longer fit who you were becoming and about getting ready. This is the reason why. If you are carrying extra baggage – your schedule is already cluttered, or your credit cards are already maxed out, you don't have the capacity to take on something else.

This is why knowing your "why," is important. Because once you know your why, you'll know what must go in your life to make room for what is to come.

But first things, first. You've got to get that vision on paper so you can look at it until it becomes so real to your subconscious that you can't help but move towards it.

Create the highest grandest vision for your life because you become what you believe.

Oprah Winfrey

One of the best ways to move towards the visions you and dreams you have is to make a vision board. If you have never done so before, check out this YouTube video on how and why to make one (www.youtube.com/watch?v=9b8DJQCOtkU). For those of you who may think this is "New Agey" or "hocus pocus" let me remind you from our focus scriptures that God basically gives Joshua a "vision board" by laying out exact parameters of the Promised Land.

Also, for most major characters in the Bible (i.e., Sarah and Abraham), God provides a "vision (board)" for what God promises them. For example, we could argue that God gave Abram and Sarah "vision boards" to help them remember the ultimate destiny He had for their lives. God told Abram to go and look at the stars in the sky to see how numerous his descendants would be. (Genesis 22: 16 – 18). Sara's name was changed from Sarai (Princess) to Sarah (Mother of Nations) so that she would have a constant reminder of what God intended for her.

If God provided a "vision" of what these major biblical characters would become, then there is no reason to believe that getting a vision for ourselves is out of reach.

So, go ahead and prayerfully make that vision board.

Go all out and see what God can do with someone who is bold enough to dream big.

Vision is a picture of the future that produces passion.

Bill Hybels

PRAYER STARTER:

Lord, help me to see the grand vision You have for my life. Help me to do what is necessary so I can cooperate with You to bring it to pass. I want to "play full out." I want to be like the faithful servants in Matthew 25 who took what was given to them and multiplied it for the Master's use. Thank you in advance for all that You are about to do with and through me for Your glory. In Jesus' name, amen.

JOURNAL QUESTIONS:

1) What is God saying to you through the Bible verse and the devotional?

2) How can you implement this step and move one step closer to your goal/resolution/promise?

3) What may hinder you in taking this step and how will you get around it?

4) How will you celebrate/acknowledge when you've taken this step (i.e., post on Facebook; share with a friend)?

5) If you didn't do this step, why or why not?

6) Identify what you need to address or resolve to accomplish this step, the support you may need, and when you'll begin addressing this.

STEP 4

Know Your Why

IF YOU AREN'T CLEAR ABOUT YOUR "WHY" YOU WILL QUIT WHEN THE CHALLENGES COME BECAUSE GOING BACK WILL SEEM EASIER

DAILY BIBLE READING

Joshua 1: 10 — 17

KEY MEMORY VERSE(S):

[6] Be strong and courageous, because you will lead these people to inherit the land I swore to their ancestors to give them.

(Joshua 1:6 NIV)

DEVOTIONAL:

A cluttered scheduled or maxed out bank account doesn't mean that you should forget about your vision. Most researchers tell us that the "why" behind your vision can help you dream big, get a vision, begin to move towards your dreams and endure the challenges that come along the way.[3] Your "why" behind the vision will also serve as motivation to help you get in position to let go of what you need to and do what you need to do to move forward, especially on days when it is easier to give up.

---

[3] Renee Warren, "Why Discovering Your 'Why' Is the No. 1 Business Move," *Entrepreneur*, March 23, 2015. Accessed March 15, 2017. https://www.entrepreneur.com/article/243737

When you know your 'why' then your 'what' has more impact, because you're working towards your purpose.

Michael Jr.

So, let's talk about your "why" – what it is in general and how to use it to help you to get ready and to move towards your vision. Your "why" is simply the reason "why" you want to accomplish your dream. Your "why" is also more than money or status. According to Forbes Contributor Margie Warrell, your "why" is based on four questions:

1) What inspires you/what makes you come alive/where do you feel the fullest?

2) What are your innate strengths? For example, are you are natural communicator, helper, teacher, etc.?

(To take a free test that will help you discover your innate strengths, go to www.viame.org.)

3) Where do you add the greatest value? At home? At work? Helping Friends?

4) When you come to the end of your life, how do you want to be remembered?[4]

The main reason to know your "why" is that more than anything else, your "why" is your primary motivator to accomplish anything and the best way to connect with others who are likeminded. In fact, researchers have discovered that people who are crystal clear about their

---

[4] Margie Warrell, ""Do You Know Your "Why?" 4 Questions To Find Your Purpose," *Forbes Magazine*, October 30, 2013, https://www.forbes.com/sites/margiewarrell/2013/10/30/know-your-why-4-questions-to-tap-the-power-of-purpose/#344bd97173ad. Accessed February 14, 2018.

"why" are able to effectively communicate it with others to achieve unbelievable success.[5]

Now that you have your "why" and you've begun to deal with some of your fears, make a physical representation of your vision and display it somewhere you can see it. This will help your subconscious mind stimulate your faith, so you can begin to work towards your dreams (Habakkuk 2:2).

> *When you know your "why," you'll know your way.*
>
> **Michael Hyatt**

Now that you have your vision board or some statement that is posted for you to see daily, you also should have on it some statement or picture to remind you of your "why," begin to move. Once these are in place to help you move towards your vision, you can begin using the Stretch Yourself One Step At A Time process to take one step at a time to accomplish anything you wish to succeed.

PRAYER STARTER:

> *Lord, help me to know why you have put me on this planet and what you have called me to do. Help me to connect my purpose to Your grander vision of bringing about the kingdom of God and of helping others to know you better. Use me to help contribute to the flourishing of all people. Let my life be an*

---

[5] Naptali Hoff, "Know Your Why," *Huffington Post*, March 21, 2016. Accessed March 15, 2017. https://www.huffingtonpost.com/naphtali-hoff/know-your-why_b_9512688.html

answer to someone's prayers, even my ancestors and my enemies. And let it be an example for those who come behind me. In Jesus' name, amen.

JOURNAL QUESTIONS:

1) What is God saying to you through the Bible verse and the devotional?

2) How can you implement this step and move one step closer to your goal/resolution/promise?

3) What may hinder you in taking this step and how will you get around it?

4) How will you celebrate/acknowledge when you've taken this step (i.e., post on Facebook; share with a friend)?

5) If you didn't do this step, why or why not?

6) Identify what you need to address or resolve to accomplish this step, the support you may need, and when you'll begin addressing this.

STEP 5

Stretch Yourself
One Step
At A Time

GET OUT OF YOUR COMFORT ZONE AND TAKE ONE
ESSENTIAL STEP AT A TIME TO ACHIEVE YOUR GOAL

DAILY BIBLE READING:

Deuteronomy 7: 17 — 26

KEY MEMORY VERSE(S):

[3] I will give you every place where you set your foot, as I
promised Moses. [4] Your territory will extend from the desert
to Lebanon, and from the great river, the Euphrates—all the
Hittite country—to the Mediterranean Sea in the west.
(Joshua 1:3-4 NIV)

DEVOTIONAL:

Many of us who have been overloaded with too many roles
and responsibilities either at work, home and/or church, are
especially prone to multitasking and wearing ourselves out
even more than we think we are. So, I thought it important
to remind us all about the dangers of multitasking,
especially how multitasking sets us up for failing to achieve
anything of lasting value in the quickest amount of time. As I
wrote in Step 3, recent studies have found that even though
it may seem to help us achieve much more in a shorter time,
multitasking actually reduces our productivity level by 40%!

Yes!!! A whopping 40 % — Wow! that's almost half the full capacity of our potential to be productive. This means that multitasking means that when focusing on more than one task at a time, we almost *double the time* required to complete each one!

Here are some other alarming facts about multitasking that we need to be reminded of again. Multitasking in the real sense:

- Damages our brains by exerting so much pressure on them;

- Destroys our ability to know what is important and what isn't; therefore making us dumb;

- Makes us prone to cheating and cutting corners;

- Makes us think that the so-called "productivity" tools are helping us when actually they aren't;

- Lowers the quality of our work output by causing us to be sloppy in its execution;

- Reduces the cognitive ability to make connections between what we are learning and what we are doing or what we were doing before then; and

- Requires even more from us in terms of workload and coordination

* Remember – multitasking reduces our productivity by almost half.[6]

As renowned New York Times best-selling author and productivity specialist, Michael Hyatt has argued one sure route to failure in accomplishing one's goals is to set and try to accomplish too many goals all at once each year. Simply

---

[6] Julie Neidlinger, "The Horrifying Truth About Multitasking," CoSchedule Blog, November 19, 2014, https://coschedule.com/blog/multitasking-and-productivity/

put, the greatest danger of multitasking and focusing (or trying to focus) on too many things at once can best be summed up by the saying, "Man/Woman who chases two rabbits at the same time catches neither."[7]

Don't try to overhaul your life overnight. Instead, focus on making one small change at a time. Over time, those small changes will add up to big transformation. Don't give up!

Anonymous

So, why then do we think that to succeed, we must multitask? Especially those of us who are of the household of God? I have identified three main reasons: First, we try to make sure that we are keeping up with everyone else's life, so we try to be excellent at everything all at once without taking into consideration our life circumstances, gifts, aptitudes, or talents for doing certain things.

Second, uninformed, multitasking church leaders suggest and preach that we should be super busy all the time as proof of our devotion to God. Third, we want it all and we want it now.

---

[7] Michael Hyatt, "Navigate Your Way to Success in 2018: 5 Blunders that Could Shipwreck Your Goals (and How to Avoid Them)," [Free, Limited Webinar], December 12, 2018.

A flower does not think about competing against others. It just blooms.

Anonymous

Underneath it all is a mad rush to prove to someone, anyone, that we are "keeping up with the Jones" and that we are significant. We do not want anyone to think that we do not have faith, so we run, run, run. At the heart of it all is that in our microwavable – "name it, claim it;" "blab it, grab it;" "sow a seed today and reap your harvest it in a week" mentality and practice of the faith, we fail to acknowledge that it is through faith and patience we inherit the promises of God (Hebrews 6:13).

Also, because many of us are unfamiliar with either farming or gardening, we do not know there is often a period, sometimes a great period of time, between sowing and reaping. There is also a lot of hard work in each step – preparing the ground to receive the seed, watering, fertilizing, weeding and reaping. Simply put, planting seed and getting the fruit of it, is not like going to the store handing over our money and immediately receiving what we pay for. It takes time, naturally, to reap from a natural garden flowers that maintain their beauty and fragrance, and fruits and vegetables that taste and are as nutritious as God intended.

The truth is by trying to "keep up," in actuality we are engaging in people-pleasing. We let someone else determine the vision and destiny of our lives by consulting people, especially those we think are more "in tune" with God. Rather than consulting God – the very one who created us as unique masterpieces for His purpose, not anyone else's, in the first place, we consult others to tell us how to become who God has made and ordained us to be (Ephesians 2:10).

Simply put, we don't consult God regarding whether we should accept the vision, the responsibilities or the challenges that others lay out for us. So, we take it all on, trying to become excellent multitaskers so that we can "obtain favor with God and humans (Luke 2:52)."

We keep running around like chickens with our heads off — multitasking and trying to keep others pleased, all the while never getting daily God-given instruction for the task at hand that is in alignment with God's vision for our lives. So, we never achieve the productivity that God intends for us. Worse still, we get so depressed and discouraged that we just quit on our resolve to "possess our promise" by accomplishing our dreams and becoming all that God intends for us to be.

> It's only by saying "no" that we can concentrate on what's really important.
>
> **Steve Jobs**

Beloved, nothing could be further from the truth of how Scripture intends for us to live which is contrary to operating this way. The Bible states that there is a season for everything – preparation, sowing, reaping, resting (Ecclesiastes 3:1 – 14). Unlike the systems of the world that can manipulate seeds to produce crops out of their natural harvest time, God will not give us a harvest if we have only done the work of sowing without putting in the rest of it – preparation, weeding, resting, and waiting. God also will not produce His fruit out of its season and His timing(John 15: 1 – 8), No matter how fast we move; how impatient we become; or what promises the "man or woman of God" make when asking us to "sow" an offering.

This is where our problems with multitasking often start — rooted in our lack of faith and patience. See, preparation—weeding, waiting, resting, harvesting — provides great temptation to multitask because preparation often looks like nothing is happening. So we get busy creating a flutter of activity that has little to do with tending to and reaping the harvest God intends.

Why? Because at least if we are multitasking, we can prove that we are "busy," so that we can tell God and others why we can't work on moving towards what will help us achieve our goals. Furthermore, in an American society that bases our worth on what we produce and how "active" we are, it's easier to appear busy, rather than weak, lazy, vulnerable or afraid.

In this way, multitasking causes us to be like the fig tree in Matthew 21, which although it had a lot of leaves, symbolic of human-initiated activity, it had no fruit, symbolic of the work of the Holy Spirit in our lives. Fruit also represents the good works that God asks of us that are the products of our faith in God's promises and commands (Matthew 21:18–20; Ephesians 2:10). Simply put, all leaves but no fruit are simply the signs of all show and no substance.

Imagine being hungry and only having the leaves of a fruit tree to eat, rather than the fruit. When Christians only produce leaves (activity with no lasting value), it is no wonder that we have nothing to offer a spiritually hungry world. It should be no surprise that given how busy, but not fruitful, our churches and lives are, that non-believers do not participate in churches. Could it be that they see our busy, but fruitless churches and lives as no different than the world in that many churches work folks to death and really only want new members to take over the work regular attendees no longer want or are able to do? Could it be that because we have nothing more to feed them with spiritually than motivational speeches and emotional, but Spiritless worship, they refuse to attend because what their souls truly desire is the sincere milk of the word of God" and an encounter with the Power and Presence of God(1 Peter 2:2)?

So how do we not fall into the trap of multitasking and being too impatient with the process? What can we do to make sure that we are "fruitful" rather than busy?

We set a few big goals a year in alignment with our vision. Then we take steps just outside of our comfort zone to achieve them. Yes, we'll move slower; but as with all people of faith, we will find that through faith and patience, we can inherit the promises, the dreams God intends for us.

How do we begin?

Here again, Joshua and some contemporary experts provide a path. In Joshua 1:3, God spoke to Joshua that He was giving to him every place "he sets his foot on." Another way to think of this is God saying, "Joshua, every place you walk on, I will give it to you." When we think of walking, we know that to be successful we must take one step at a time. (I guess someone should have told all those persons doing studies on multitasking that God had given the instructions about accomplishing goals long ago; and here it is: stretch and take one step at a time.)

In fact, Michael Hyatt argues that if we are going to achieve our dreams (possess our promise), we should set no more than 7 to 10 goals a year, and then select no more than 2 – 3 goals to focus on every 3 – 4 months. He further suggests that to set great goals, we need to review each goal based on the three zones of goal setting – the *Comfort Zone*, the

Discomfort Zone, and the *Delusional Zone*.

The Comfort zone requires little to no effort on your part.

The *Delusional Zone* is just that – delusional (i.e. that I don't care how many promises the infomercial makes. You will not lose 50 lbs. in a month without cutting off your head.).

The greatest danger for most of us is not that we aim too high and we miss it, but we aim too low and reach it.

Anonymous

This leaves us with the last which is the *Discomfort Zone*. A goal set in the *Discomfort Zone* is just strenuous enough to cause you to feel fearful, uncertain or full of doubt. It is also the one that you could achieve if you would be willing to identify and take the small but essential steps you need to take to achieve *Discomfort Zone*.[8] Goals in the process of determining your *Discomfort Zone* goal and then breaking these into small essential steps I define as "Stretch Yourself One Step At A Time."

Once you have identified your *Discomfort Zone* goals (i.e., those that will require you to stretch.) Then break these down into the small, but essential steps you need to achieve your goal is by making them SMART steps. SMART steps are the small incremental steps that will help you accomplish your *Discomfort Zone* goals and that are:

S - Specific: What exactly is the very first step of any action/learning/goal identified?

---

[8] Hyatt, ""Navigate Your Way to Success in 2018: 5 Blunders that Could Shipwreck Your Goals (and How to Avoid Them)."

M - Measurable: For what you have listed in "Specific," how have you determined how you will measure your progress?

A - Achievable: Is the initial step possible to achieve? (if not, its probably Delusional. You need to review your process and reset your Discomfort Zone goal.)

R - Reasonable: How reasonable is it that what you're saying you're going to do can be done, at this time?

T - Time-Oriented: By when, exactly will you complete the first (or this) step of the Discomfort Zone goal you identified?

The secret of success is discipline which is built by consistently performing small acts of courage one step at a time.

Anonymous

Also, if you really want to give yourself a boost in conquering your fears, doubts and uncertainties then you should boost your goal setting approach by linking inner and outer goals (i.e., your "why" and your feelings). While the "Stretch Yourself One Step At A Time" process helps you determine and work your way through your outer-directed goals, you can put your emotions to work for you through visualization. Visualization is simply using your imagination in partnership with your feelings and all of your senses – sight, hearing, smell, touch and taste, to experience what it is you desire. The process of visualization is used widely in every field you can imagine from such areas as pain management, psychology, medicine, sports and business. Adults, adolescents and children have all benefitted from its techniques. It has also been the subject of many professional studies[9]

> *I would visualize things coming to me. It would just make me feel better. Visualization works if you work hard. That's the thing. You can't just visualize and go eat a sandwich.*
>
> **Jim Carrey**

To begin the process of visualization, take a few deep breaths to relax yourself. Then imagine what it feels like to achieve your Discomfort Zone Goal even though you have not achieved it yet. Practice this process as often as you can. Push aside any thoughts that try to tell you why you can't. Just imagine that you have ALREADY accomplished what you desire. Now begin to "act as if" you already have your goal completed and expect that it is on the way. Another way to think of this is to recall Jesus' admonition from Mark 11:23-24:

> [23] "Truly I tell you, if anyone says to this mountain, 'Go, throw yourself into the sea,' and does not doubt in their heart but believes that what they say will happen, it will be done for them. [24] Therefore I tell you, whatever you ask for in prayer, believe that you have received it, and it will be yours.

---

[9] ibigail Brenner, "The Benefits of Creative Visualization: How Practice In Your Mind Makes Perfect," Psychology Today (June 25, 2016). Accessed April 5, 2018. https://www.psychologytoday.com/us/blog/in-flux/201606/the-benefits-creative-visualization.

An example of Getting a Vision and pursuing it through with the process of Stretching and Taking It One Step At A Time would be:

- Vision: To earn a college degree or a certification as soon you realize a cogent need for it (Considering that age doesn't matter).

- Vision Board Picture: Consider taking a picture of a model that looks like you in a cap and gown or photoshopping yourself in a cap and gown; making a sample diploma with your name on it; and/or doing what you will be able to do once you have that degree.

- Stretch Yourself One Step At A Time: After reviewing information online, make an appointment to go and/or speak with the admissions offices of the colleges/training program that you are interested in within 2 weeks.

- Imagine how you will feel when you achieve that goal (i.e. graduating) and feel like it now: Feel proud, happy, excited, like you're able to do anything… NOW.

- Begin to clear your schedule so you can begin and finish school.

Beloved, do yourself a favor: Don't just answer the questions that are a part of this step's or the previous two steps' devotionals. Make a date with yourself to Get A Vision (make that board), Get Clear on Your "Why," Stretch Yourself One Step At A Time, and Feel/Act As If You Already Have It (i.e., it's on the way) as often as you can. Remember that God often takes us step by step, or as it says in the reading for today from Deuteronomy 7, little by little. Why does God often allow us to achieve our goals and dreams little by little? Because if we tried dealing with everything all at once, we would be overwhelmed and turn back or burnout (Deuteronomy 7:22).

Even more important than getting our vision and stretching yourself one step at a time, we need to remember that all of this is useless without Step 7: which is to ponder and practice the Presence of God. Just as our dreams and visions must come from God, these strategies will only work when we remember that God has not left us to ourselves to implement them. We seek God's Presence and guidance in achieving our goals so that we will be clear and guided that our victories will not be won in our own strength but by the wisdom, leadership and empowerment from God's spirit.

In my daily walk with Him, He gives me victory as He teaches me how to abide."

Judy Harrell

PRAYER STARTER:

Lord, please give me /re-ignite in me that grand vision you have for my life, something so AWESOME that it can only be accomplished by You working in and through me. Dear Lord, please give me the courage to Stretch Myself One Step At A Time; to break the vision down into appropriate REASONABLE steps that will help move me closer and closer to the outcome you have for me. Help me to create something that will remind me of Your Vision and

Why I am doing it. Let me feel now I like I will when it is accomplished. Please don't let the enemy, friends, families or even me, talk me out of working with You and surrendering to You to accomplish any of this. In Jesus' precious name. Amen.

JOURNAL QUESTIONS:

1) What is God saying to you through the Bible verse and the devotional?

2) How can you implement this step and move one step closer to your goal/resolution/promise?

3) What may hinder you in taking this step and how will you get around it?

4) How will you celebrate/acknowledge when you've taken this step (i.e., post on Facebook; share with a friend)?

5) If you didn't do this step, why or why not?

6) Identify what you need to address or resolve to accomplish this step, the support you may need, and when you'll begin addressing this.

STEP 6

Get A New Vision of Yourself

YOU CAN BECOME YOUR BEST VERSION BY GETTING A NEW VISION.

DAILY BIBLE READING:

Exodus 17: 8 - 16

KEY MEMORY VERSE(S):

[5] No one shall be able to stand against you all the days of your life. As I was with Moses, so I will be with you; I will not fail you or forsake you. [6] Be strong and courageous; for you shall put this people in possession of the land that I swore to their ancestors to give them.

(Joshua 1:5-6 NIV)

DEVOTIONAL:

You are stronger, smarter, and more resilient than you think. You are capable of achieving far more than you believe. You were meant for greatness – like all of those who have achieved it.

But it takes persistence. It takes determination. It takes facing your fears and doing that which is hard and necessary, instead of what is quick and easy. It takes skipping the mythical shortcuts & using your imagination as a map and preview of life's coming attractions.

Zero Dean

When someone asks you who you are? What do you say? Most of us typically describe ourselves by our roles – son/daughter, parent, occupation, spouse/partner, etc. Often, many of us <u>only</u> describe ourselves by one of the many roles we hold. What a shame!

The issue with describing ourselves by our roles is that it doesn't take into consideration that when the current roles end, many of us are prone to feeling lost. When the situation ends – the job is over, the children are grown, the marriage is over — we literarily become handicapped because we never cared to know who we really are based on who God made us to be. More than this, because many of us only see and know ourselves by our roles; we experience very stiff opposition from ourselves and others when we try to transcend that level or dared to see ourselves as having the capacity of being more.

Whenever we describe ourselves only in relation to something or someone else, our identity is unstable because it rests on something that is only temporal – prone to failures and flaws; and very finicky. Because we never knew our true identity independent of our relationship to someone or something else, not only do we question our identity, we question our worth. More than that, because many of us only know ourselves by our roles, we have a problem transcending them or seeing ourselves as capable of being or doing more than we are currently.

So why do we need a new vision of ourselves to be the best version of ourselves? Because our "real identity," the true essence of who we are, must be in alignment with who God has created us to be, not based on our relation to anything or anyone else. When our identity is grounded in who God has created us to be, then our worth, especially in our own eyes, is determined by who God says we are rather than by anyone or anything else.

You are bigger than your defined role, and you are much more than your job title. Play your part – transcend your job title, BE A HERO."

Luke Bucklin, Sierra Bravo Corporation

When we are clear about our God-given identity and value, then we are better able to occupy a variety of roles on our way to achieving all that God desires for us. In this way, our past roles have no way of limiting us because we can reach for more based on what God has put in us and the opportunities God places before us. The reality of us achieving our dreams is no longer limited by how we or others see us. We can move confidently into the future because we understand that with every opportunity God is revealing more of who God has created us to be.

Joshua experienced and understood what it meant to be a person of varying roles. The first encounter with Joshua in the Scriptures shows that Joshua (Hoshea) is mentioned as one of the Israelites who was a slave under Pharaoh. After the exodus from Egypt, Joshua was sent with others to spy out the Promised Land (Numbers 13:8). Before the spies were sent out, we see that Moses changed Hoshea's name to Joshua (Numbers 13:16).

Have you ever wondered why on earth would Moses change Hoshea's name to "Joshua"? Both names refer to "salvation." Hoshea means "salvation" while Joshua means "The Lord Is My Salvation." So why the sudden name change?

Many commentators believe Moses changed the name of his assistant "Hoshea" to "Joshua" to openly signify that it was the Lord who would provide salvation for Joshua and not

Joshua himself. The name change was also to also signify that although Hoshea belonged to his father Nun's house (lineage), he is from now on second-in-command only to Moses. By changing his name, Moses was positioning Joshua for his ultimate purpose – leading the children of Israel to possess the land that the Lord had promised to their ancestors by the Lord's wisdom, strength and might.

This is a significant insight for this study. It provides some insight into how much influence our parents wield over who we think we are or who we think we can be. There are quite a few people who are held down because of a faulty belief system they inherited from their parents or communities.

As a matter of fact, fears, doubts and limiting beliefs about who we can be most often come from the people we love and trust. From our superiors or parents, it is obviously expressed as a negligent or unkind word spoken by them over the child or young adult. It can even come from parents and superiors, who thinking that they are protecting us, "define our limits" by reminding us to "stay in our place" or that "people like us don't do things like that."

As a matter of fact, fears, doubts and limiting beliefs about who we can become sometimes come from the people we love and trust.

Felicia LaBoy

I can vividly recall an example from Civil Rights' icon and U.S. Congressman John Lewis' life of how parents and grandparents can limit their children and grandchildren unintentionally by trying to keep them safe. Lewis says that he had always thought that segregation was wrong and that someone ought to do something about it.

Every time he mentioned to his mother that someone ought to speak up or do something about this injustice, his mother had told him "not to get in the way and to always stay out of trouble." Advice that Congressman Lewis clearly has not followed. In fact, he has created a niche for himself by making it his mission to "always get in the way" and to "get into GOOD trouble."[10]

How did he make the shift? Here is his inspiring story. From humble beginnings, Congressman Lewis always thought that he was more than his family or society thought of him and who he could be. From all accounts, foundational to his belief was his commitment to be of service to God. In fact, Congressman Lewis' aspirations were to be a pastor, not a politician. Most of all, his driving passion was to do something to end segregation and secure equal rights and access for all.

Because of his desire to be a pastor, Congressman Lewis left his small town to attend Bible college in Nashville. While there, he got involved in those things that stirred his passion for civil rights. The chief of them was nonviolent resistance against segregation. Later, he found a mentor – Rev. Dr. Martin Luther King, Jr., because he was bold enough to inquire of Dr. King how he might be of service in the fight to end segregation.

It can be argued that Congressman Lewis became who he is today because of two things. First, his identity and security were based on his relationship with God, not on who others said he was or could be. Second, he pursued his mission of securing equal rights and access for all by being bold

[10] Taryn Finley, "Congressman John Lewis Urges Bates Grads To Get Into 'Good Trouble,'" *Black Voices* [blog], May 31, 2016, https://www.huffingtonpost.com/entry/congressman-john-lewis-urges-bates-grads-to-get-into-good-trouble_us_574d9587e4b055bb1172a3ce

enough to step into a wide variety of roles – Student, Freedom Rider, Integrator, Congressman.

How about you? Do you believe you can transcend your family? Your neighborhood? Are you bold enough to redefine yourself based on your relationship with God and on a guiding mission that is liberating for others?

Each of our roles serves as a snapshot in time of what we are capable of at a particular moment. Rather than define us, they are preparation for the skills we'll need to possess our promise.

Felicia LaBoy

Not only was Joshua a slave and a spy. Joshua was a soldier—an army general/commander. (Exodus 17: 8 – 16). With all his accolades, Joshua is also described as Moses' servant (Exodus 24:13). Joshua was also identified to be a worshipper (Exodus 33: 7 – 11).

As we can see by reading Joshua's life history prior to his commissioning by God to lead the Israelites into the Promised Land, Joshua's roles as slave, spy, army general/commander, assistant and worshipper were not his identity. Each role served as an opportunity to enhance and highlight Joshua's talents, strengths, abilities. They provided a snapshot of what Joshua was capable of at a <u>particular</u> moment in time.

This is a critical observation because when we assume that our role is our identity, then often we have a hard time letting go of this role well beyond its time. A good example of this are parents who refuse to let their children grow up and become responsible adults. For these parents, they continually interfere in how their adult children conduct their affairs and meddle in every aspect of their lives.

Another example of this are people who stay in either job or volunteer positions well past their prime because they "don't know what they will do with themselves" if they were to quit, even though they are tired and/or becoming increasingly ineffective.

Every next level of your life will demand a different you.

Leonardo DeCaprio

All of Joshua's roles also served as preparation for his destiny to lead the children of Israel into the Promised Land. If we were to read through the entire book of Joshua, we would learn that Joshua uses all the skills of spy, military leader, servant, and worshipper to lead the children of Israel into possessing the Promised Land. Is it possible that God has been using the various roles that you have occupied as a training ground for God's ultimate plan for your life?

In addition to not only describing ourselves by our roles, many of us limit ourselves by our age, physical limitations or inabilities. Because we choose to believe the "too old, too young, too poor, too fat, etc.," lies, we wrongly assume that God couldn't possibly want us to pursue that dream burning in our heart. Beloved, nothing could be further from this truth. Let's look at Joshua our example again.

It had been 40 years since Joshua had been to Canaan and tasted the fruit of the land. It had also been over 40 years after he conquered the Amalekites. Even if he wanted to fight, it's been long time since he had. By all indications

Joshua was an old man. Some commentators believe God commissioned Joshua to lead the children of Israel to war against Canaan when Joshua was at 80 years old. By all indications Joshua should have been ready for retirement, not some new mission when God comes to him in Joshua 1.

Sounds strange?

Read that again.

Joshua was 80 YEARS OLD when God told him to go get what God had already given to him.

> *We are not limited by our age, physical limitations or inabilities. If God says we can, then we are well-able to possess our promise.*
>
> **Felicia LaBoy**

So beloved, a question that is resonating with me right now is that what made Joshua or someone like Congressman Lewis believe that they could accomplish their dreams? What inspired them to do even more than their background, their former roles or their age suggested? More importantly for us who are working to become unstuck, what gave Joshua the courage to move from the "second chair" to be leader of a mighty and conquering nation?

I think it was Congressman Lewis' and Joshua's views of themselves which were grounded on God's view of them. It was the fact that they knew they were more than their roles or "so-called limitations." What allowed them to possess their promise was that they were clear about their God-given identities and value which was revealed and affirmed during the time spent in the presence of God (Joshua 1:5 – 7).

Furthermore, from all available accounts Joshua was convinced of the promises of God. Whether as a middle-aged man or as an old man. If God said that Joshua could, then Joshua would move forward in possessing his promise knowing that "with God all things are possible" (Mark 10:27).

Simply put, Joshua was convinced of his success because he knew that "the Lord was his salvation" long before the Apostle Paul wrote:

> [13] *I can do all things [which He has called me to do] through Him who strengthens and empowers me [to fulfill His purpose—I am self-sufficient in Christ's sufficiency; I am ready for anything and equal to anything through Him who infuses me with inner strength and confident peace.] (Philippians 4:13 AMP).*

Beloved, if we are going to possess our promises (i.e., the dreams in our heart), we are going to have to believe that we are more than our roles and/or our so called "limitations." We are going to have to spend some time with God, so we can be sure of our identity and our value beyond our roles. More importantly, we are going to have to start seeing ourselves the way that God sees us – well able and more than conquerors.

> *Too many of us are not living our dreams because we are living our fears.*
>
> **Les Brown**

We are going to have to know that if God says we can, then we can begin to take steps that move us towards accomplishing our dreams. To do that, we are going to have to take time to reflect on God and meditate on the promises of God found in God's Word.

PRAYER STARTER:

Lord, it is hard for me to understand how I have allowed myself to be shaped either by my roles or by how others define me. This has caused me to not know or appreciate who you have called and made me to be. It's made me not know who I am and whose I am beyond what I do. Please let me know and value myself based on who you have made me to be and your plan for my life. Help me to appreciate who I am beyond my roles. Amen.

JOURNAL QUESTIONS:

1) What is God saying to you through the Bible verse and the devotional?

2) How can you implement this step and move one step closer to your goal/resolution/promise?

3) What may hinder you in taking this step and how will you get around it?

4) How will you celebrate/acknowledge when you've taken this step (i.e., post on Facebook; share with a friend)?

5) If you didn't do this step, why or why not?

6) Identify what you need to address or resolve to accomplish this step, the support you may need, and when you'll begin addressing this.

STEP 7

Pondering and Practicing the Presence of God

YOU ONLY WILL BE ENCOURAGED AND STRENGTHENED FOR THE JOURNEY AHEAD IN THE PRESENCE OF GOD

DAILY BIBLE READING:

Exodus 33:12 - 17

KEY MEMORY VERSE(S):

[5] No one shall be able to stand against you all the days of your life. As I was with Moses, so I will be with you; I will not fail you or forsake you. [6] Be strong and courageous; for you shall put this people in possession of the land that I swore to their ancestors to give them.

(Joshua 1:5-6 NIV)

DEVOTIONAL:

It seems to me that one of the most important Spiritual Exercises that we can engage in is to Spend Time in God's Presence. When I am aware that I am connected to God, I have peace, hope and the spiritual strength that I need for whatever the day brings me.

Dale Fletcher

If you find yourself a bit irritated or overwhelmed, it's a sign that you're spending less time with the Lord and too much with this world."

Anonymous

I am the vine; you are the branches. If you remain in me and I in you, you will bear much fruit; apart from me you can do nothing.

Jesus (John 15:5)

In his book *Secrets of the Vine: Breaking Through to Abundance*, Bruce Wilkerson argues that there are four levels in terms of being engaged in ministry with and for God, which he refers to as "fruit-bearing:"

- The level of bearing *no fruit*

- The level of bearing *fruit*

- The level of bearing *more fruit,* and

- The level of bearing *much fruit.*

Wilkerson states that while each level is more and more productive than the preceding one, God's ultimate desire is that we bear "much fruit." The only sure way to bearing "much fruit" is abiding with God and allowing God to do His good work in and through us. In bearing much fruit, we move beyond asking God to bless our ministry efforts to surrendering to God's purpose for our lives and joining God in the work God desires by becoming co-laborers with God.

Wilkerson contends that the greatest tragedy in the church today is that almost 50% of Christians are either bearing just a little or sadly enough no fruit at all for the kingdom of God. Sadder still he estimates that about only 5% bear the kind of fruit in their lives that Jesus speaks of when he equates bearing "much fruit" as the mark of mature discipleship in (John 15:8) [11] In fact, Jesus boldly and clearly stated that the only way to bear fruit, especially if we desired to attain the level of "much fruit" is to abide in Him.

While it is very easy to read and claim that we are following the mandates of John 15:1 – 8, the reality is that the process of abiding with God is anything but easy. Not only do we have more things that clutter our schedules and overwhelm our souls, many of us are rather addicted to busyness due to multitasking and people-pleasing as we have discussed in previous devotions.

Many of us are also addicted to striving and achieving so much so that it is wearing us and everyone else around us out – especially at church. Even more so, there are quite a few of us who, because of an unhealthy dose of being overly responsible, never take the time to assess whether something is ours to do or not. We forget that we have a Savior whose name is Jesus, not (fill in your name). And we fail to trust that even if we don't do it and things go horribly wrong, God will be with us even in the midst of the trouble, working it out for our good and His glory (Romans 8:28-39).

Jesus didn't do it all. Jesus didn't meet every need. He left people waiting in line to be healed. He left one town to preach to another. He hid away to pray. He got tired. He never interacted with the vast majority of people on the planet. He spent thirty years in training and only three years in ministry. He did not

---

[11] Bruce Wilkerson, *Secrets of the Vine: Breaking Through to Abundance* (Breakthrough Series Book 2) (p. 25 - 27). The Crown Publishing Group. Kindle Edition.

try to do it all. And yet, He did everything God asked Him to do.

Kevin DeYoung

For Christians, even more problematic is that although many of us claim to have our "quiet time" or "devotional time" with God, these are little more than just "business meetings" with God where we merely read/skim through a passage of Scripture, say a prayer for us and those closest to us, and/or ask God to bless our day and our efforts. Most often, even if we have set aside a time and place to "be with God," our minds are distracted and ferried far away to somewhere else.

Not only that, even when we disclose our troubles and problems to God during these times, we often end up spending more time fellowshipping with our problems than with God. We constantly replay them over and over in our mind trying to come up with a solution that we can make happen. Rather than truly and honestly fellowshipping with God and getting His perspective and guidance, we focus only on how we think our prayers ought to be answered. We forget that when we pray about issues that we should present them confidently to God knowing that God has the best response to our problem.

The battle of prayer is against two things in the earthlies: wandering thoughts, and lack of intimacy with God's character as revealed in His word. Neither can be cured at once, but they can be cured by discipline.

Oswald Chambers

The truth is that most of this distraction during our quiet times comes because of two faulty mindsets that many believers have accepted. First, even though we say that we are people of the covenant, many of us act like it's a contract we have with God.

We believe that if and only if we do our part, then God is "required" to fulfill His. So, we make sure that we attend church, give, help people and try to be nice believing that these are the requirements to a blessed life.

We forget that God is in a convenantal, not contractual, relationship with us. We can do nothing covenantal more to be accepted and loved or blessed – Jesus has finished this work on the cross. God is committed to us, not because of what we do or who we are. God is committed to us because He has purposed within Himself to do so and sees us under the blood of Jesus Christ. This is not to say that sin doesn't have consequences. It does. It is to say that our maturing in the faith is determined by how we live out and live into being beloved sons and daughters of God. We are simply living into who God already says we are.

> *It's not the law of religion nor the principles of morality that define our highways and pathways to God; only by the Grace of God are we led and drawn, to God. It is His grace that conquers a multitude of flaws and in that grace, there is only favor. Favor is not achieved; favor is received.*
>
> **C. JoyBell C.**

Most of us, whether we want to admit it or not, can agree that there have been times when we haven't been at our best and God has shown grace and mercy on us. In our covenantal relationship with God the emphasis is on the goodness and grace of God. In contractual relationships the emphasis is on us and our performance. Everything in the Bible, especially in the New Testament, points to this radical love and grace of God towards us. Before we could do anything to get right with Him, God already makes provision for us to be "right" because of Jesus' finished work on the cross (Romans 5:8).

The second faulty belief system that many of us carry along into our relationship with him is that God's intention for our lives is for us to remain servants to him throughout our entire relationship with him.

Beloved, nothing could be further from the truth. In John 15, the chapter in which Jesus explains the steps needed for our fruitfulness, Jesus makes us know that the ultimate description of who we are and who we should strive to be in our relationship with God is to become a "friend."

> *The very moment I may, if I desire, become the friend of God.*
>
> **St. Augustine**

Friends, not servants. Let that sink in for a minute.

Now think of how we relate to friends. First and foremost, look at it from the perspective of how we react when our friends send us a letter, card, email or text. We don't skim through it like we do other correspondence. We take our time to savor it. We look to see what may be behind the message. Moreover, because we know that our wellbeing is ultimately at the heart of any correspondence between us and our friends, we are open to their insight, even if it means critique and rebuke.

This is not only how we treat mere written correspondence. How do we act when we are in the presence of our best friends? First, many of us, schedule time to be with them. Even when we are busy, if they call, we readily pick up the phone to talk. We allow ourselves to simply be – vulnerable, emotional, quiet, foolish.

Second, when we are in their presence, we speak with them face-to-face. We do not dominate the conversation and then say "Goodbye" without listening to anything they have to say. We enter into dialogue, not monologue with them. With major decisions, we ask for their input and their guidance.

I'm convicted about my time with God; what about you?

But there is hope.

In the devotional reading for today, we learn that as Moses' assistant, Joshua learns that the true source and strength of Moses' leadership is generated in the quality of the time spent in the Tent of Meeting, where Moses spoke with God face-to-face. Along with Joshua, when we take the time to study passages of Scriptures about Moses' time with God in the Tent of meeting, we also learn that it was Moses' spoke to God and God spoke to Moses, as "one to a friend" (Exodus 33: 11).

More importantly, we discover that after Moses' left his "quiet time" with God; Joshua, as a young man, stayed on. Why? Most commentators make two important contributions to our discussion about Joshua's time in the Tent of Meeting after Moses leaves.

The friend of God must not spend a day without God, [s]he must undertake no work apart from his[her] God.

Charles Spurgeon

First, they contend that by accompanying Moses' to the tent of meeting, Joshua was being discipled regarding how he should relate to God and how he should converse with God for instruction. Second, and most importantly, many commentators suggest that Joshua stayed behind because he needed to "understand God more and be saturated in God's glory" until he learned to view things from God's perspective.[12]

This is critical for our study because if we like Joshua, are going to achieve our big dreams, then we are going to have to get God's directive about how to do it and when to move and when to rest. We also will need God's companionship — not only for the assurance of victory; but for sustenance along the way.

God's promise to be with Joshua as he was with Moses was in short God's promise to be with Joshua as friend. More than vindicator, conqueror, accomplisher — friend. Wow! Imagine that. God as Joshua's friend when things got tough; when Joshua was afraid; when Joshua wanted to throw in the towel; when Joshua wanted to settle; when the people did not want to follow; and when Joshua had to stand alone. This is all easily summed up in these words of the hymn *What A Friend We Have in Jesus*:

1. What a friend we have in Jesus,

---

[12] Ephrata Ministries, "Joshua – A Young Man: Depart Not Out of the Tabernacle," *The Heartbeat of the Remnant*, July/August/September 2007, Accessed February 20, 2018. http://ephrataministries.org/remnant-2007-3Q-index.a5w

all our sins and griefs to bear!
What a privilege to carry
everything to God in prayer!
O what peace we often forfeit,
O what needless pain we bear,
all because we do not carry
everything to God in prayer.

2. Have we trials and temptations?
    Is there trouble anywhere?
    We should never be discouraged;
    take it to the Lord in prayer.
    Can we find a friend so faithful
    who will all our sorrows share?
    Jesus knows our every weakness;
    take it to the Lord in prayer.

3. Are we weak and heavy laden,
    cumbered with a load of care?
    Precious Savior, still our refuge;
    take it to the Lord in prayer.
    Do thy friends despise, forsake thee?
    Take it to the Lord in prayer!
    In his arms he'll take and shield thee;
    thou wilt find a solace there.

Faith, and hope, and patience and all the strong, beautiful, vital forces of piety are withered and dead in a prayerless life. The life of the individual believer, his personal salvation, and personal Christian graces have their being, bloom, and fruitage in prayer.

E.M. Bounds

See I think it no coincidence that a mark of the abundance that Canaan possessed was a valley where the grapes grew in such huge clusters that it took two men to carry them (Numbers 13: 23-24). Two men to signify that to accomplish great things for God requires not going it alone. The grapes to signify the fruit God produces in us. In fact, the spies named the place where they cut the grapes down the Valley of Eshkol (grape clusters). If Wilkerson is correct, then the land that Joshua spied out some 40+ years before, and where God is calling him to conquer is the valley where he would bear much fruit as symbolized by the abundance and size of grapes in the area.

To be successful, Joshua is told that he must ponder and practice the Presence of the God who had promises to be with him so that he may lay hold to the vast promise God had made.

This is a message for each of us. We too need to practice and ponder the Presence of God, what John 15 calls abiding with God, until we understand God more and are saturated with God's glory. Only then can we view our promise and every step to get there from God's perspective. We need to practice the Presence of God so that we can readily claim who we are and whose we are in the face of uncertainty and trials.

A vital key to pondering and practicing the Presence of God is to meditate on the word of God. Practical steps for doing this are found in Step 8: Take Time to Meditate on God's Promises Found in God's Word.

PRAYER STARTER:

Lord, sometimes I feel far away from You. My desire is to grow closer and closer. Help me to believe that you call me your friend; and that you want our relationship to be that of friends, not of Master and servant. Help me to remember that I can bring anything to you. Remind me that as you were with Moses and Joshua; you are with me. Remind me that without you I can do nothing; and teach me to abide with you until I understand you better, reflect Your glory and have your perspective on every aspect of my life. Produce "much fruit" in and through me. In Jesus' Name. Amen.

JOURNAL QUESTIONS:

1) What is God saying to you through the Bible verse and the devotional?

2) How can you implement this step and move one step closer to your goal/resolution/promise?

3) What may hinder you in taking this step and how will you get around it?

4) How will you celebrate/acknowledge when you've taken this step (i.e., post on Facebook; share with a friend)?

5) If you didn't do this step, why or why not?

6) Identify what you need to address or resolve to accomplish this step, the support you may need, and when you'll begin addressing this.

STEP 8

Take Time to Meditate on God's Promises and Principles Found in God's Word (the Bible)

SUCCESS GOD'S WAY IS ONLY ACHIEVED THROUGH UNDERSTANDING AND RELYING ON GOD'S PROMISES AND GOD'S PRINCIPLES.

DAILY BIBLE READING:

Psalm 119:1 - 16

KEY MEMORY VERSE(S):

[7] "Be strong and very courageous. Be careful to obey all the law my servant Moses gave you; do not turn from it to the right or to the left, that you may be successful wherever you go. [8] Keep this Book of the Law always on your lips; meditate on it day and night, so that you may be careful to do everything written in it. Then you will be prosperous and successful. [9] Have I not commanded you? Be strong and courageous. Do not be afraid; do not be discouraged, for the Lord your God will be with you wherever you go.

(Joshua 1:7-9 NIV)

DEVOTIONAL:

It is not hasty reading, but seriously meditating upon holy and heavenly truths that makes them prove sweet and profitable to the soul. It is not the bee's touching on the flowers that gathers the honey, but her abiding for a time upon them, and drawing out the sweet. It is not he that reads most, but he that meditates most on divine truth, that will prove the choicest, wisest, strongest Christian.

Joseph Hall

If you remain in me and my words remain in you, ask whatever you wish, and it will be done for you.

Jesus (John 15:7)

A 2017 research study by LifeWay Research found that while almost 87% of American households own an average of three Bibles, less than half of all Americans have actually read them. The same study found that even among Christians, over 50% did not read their Bibles on a consistent basis; with the men reading their Bibles less often than women.[13]

Why do so many of us spend more time reading other things – Facebook, Instagram and Twitter feeds, etc., when there are so many promises in the Bible that are associated with spending time reading, studying, reflecting and abiding in God's Word?

There are several answers. First, we are a nation of skimmers and this may not entirely be our fault. Several studies in the last few years report that because of the flood of information available via social media and on the web, our brains are becoming digitized. Our brains form circuits that bypass deep, slow and comprehensive reading in favor of

---

[13] Lifeway Research, *Americans Are Fond of the Bible; Don't Actually Read It,* (Nashville: Lifeway Research), April 25, 2017,

skimming – picking out key words and phrases to generate the most information at the highest speed. Also, given all the distractions of reading online either through social media or web sites, clicking, pictures, email, notifications, ads, etc. are all helping to reinforce this short-circuitry by engaging all our other senses.

In addition, online sentences tend to be short with difficult background information hyperlinked for us to choose or not. Thus, we read short articles without any pertinent background information, believing that we fully comprehend the information we access online. In this way, we are subjected to the editing and interpretation of others rather than utilizing critical thinking skills about what we are reading.[14]

Books allow you to fully explore a topic and immerse yourself in a deeper way than most media today.

Mark Zuckerberg

The cost of skimming, therefore, is that our brains, which have been trained over millennia to read by processing data in a linear fashion – i.e., reading down one page and moving from one page to the next, are now just looking for sound bites of data. The result is that we cannot comprehend at the levels we used to; and we miss key points in the texts that we read.

[14] Michael S. Rosenwald, "Serious Reading Takes A Hit from Online Scanning and Skimming Researchers Say," *The Washington Post*, April 6, 2014. Accessed February 10, 2018. https://www.washingtonpost.com/local/serious-reading-takes-a-hit-from-online-scanning-and-skimming-researchers-say/2014/04/06/088028d2-b5d2-11e3-b899-20667de76985_story.html?utm_term=.ba7686f6fda2

Simply put, although we are taking in more and more data, we are losing our ability to retain what we read. Worse still, researchers are reporting that we are losing our ability to be patient enough with longer works such as novels and works like the Bible. Whereas researchers have studied this phenomenon only as it pertains to fictional reading, this digitizing of our brains and loss of reading and comprehension skills must have implications for us as Christians regarding our abilities to patiently study and comprehend the word of God.

The other, and main issue, for us who are Christians, is that our brains have a very hard time doing what the Bible promises will bring us comfort and success – i.e., meditate and abide in the Scriptures – to read in context for deeper meaning, to ponder texts, to chew on them until they become food for our souls.

You will not get through your Christian walk of faith without studying the Bible. Everything you need in life is in God's Word. With it we find encouragement and guidance on our walk of faith.

Fritz Cherry

Beloved, the Bible is clear: if we are going to be successful, we must meditate and study our Bibles to get a better understanding of the meaning of the texts. This means studying passages of Scripture to understand them in the context by which the original audiences heard them. To do this we must be aware of the historical and cultural issues of the day.

We also need to understand that the original languages of the Bible are Hebrew and Greek. This is important because some words do not translate well from the original language into English. By not knowing the historical and cultural issues, as well as the deeper meaning behind the words we read, we miss the opportunity to gain a richer and clearer understanding of what we read. We fail to understand that all translations of the Bible are influenced by the conscious and subconscious biases of the persons translating it. More importantly, not studying the word of God for ourselves leaves us susceptible to those who would use God's word to manipulate and misinform.

> [15] *Make every effort [Do your best; Be diligent] to ·give [present] yourself to God as the kind of person he will approve. Be a worker who ·is not ashamed [or will not be shamed] and who ·uses the true teaching in the right way [correctly handles the true message/word of truth; or holds carefully to the true message/word of truth].*
>
> ### 2 Timothy 2:15 (Expanded Bible)

Truthfully beloved, meditating on the Word of God is going to take time and effort. It means that we are going to have to engage in reading, studying, contemplating the texts of the Bible. This should probably happen off-line to regenerate our brain's ability to not only read and comprehend; but to enhance our ability to linger, ponder and abide with the word of God. Simply put, for the Scriptures and other important reading, we need to go back to print.

Regardless of what we may think, researchers have discovered that comprehension, and our ability to understand and utilize the text, is better with print than online. Another way to think about this is that we must learn to become bi-literate – developing the capability to discern what can/should be read online and what should be read in print.

Rest assured, there are benefits to reading books in print that are in alignment with God's command to study and meditate over God's word. In comparing reading across digital versus print media, researchers found:

- Print reading is more "enjoyable" because printed materials are "more real" to the brain, involve more emotional processing, and cause more internalization of the material read.[15]

- When people read in print, they are better able to follow and remember the "plot line" (i.e., the order of events in the story);

- Print readers are better able to comprehend and analyze what they read better; thereby building stronger critical thinking skills;

- Research participants reported that it is easier to focus" on print and that they would be more likely to "reread" printed work[15]

With this in mind, let me offer some ways that we might get started to reflect and read God's Word to "keep this Book of the Law always on our lips; meditate on it day and night, so that we may be careful to do everything written in it in order to be prosperous and successful" (Joshua 1:8):

---

[15] Naomi Baron, "Why Digital Reading Is No Substitute for Print," *The New Republic*, July 20, 2016. Accessed March 14, 2018. https://newrepublic.com/article/135326/digital-reading-no-substitute-print

1) Purchase a PRINT Study Bible that is in a version that you can read.

   Many people have King James Version (KJV) of the Bible lying around their homes which they can neither read nor understand due to complicated and convoluted texts. This inability to understand is only compounded when we consider our poor reading and comprehension skills due to skimming.

   Furthermore, because the biblical texts are written in a time and language other than our own, it is hard for us to get the full effect of what the author is trying to convey to the original audience and then to try and apply and/or reflect on this message for our time.

   The best versions of the Bible to read for beginners are the New International Version, the New Revised Standard Version, the Common English Bible and the New Living Translation.

   The next important step is to select a Study Bible in the version that you have chosen. A Study Bible helps us bridge the gap between Biblical time and ours. It provides information that helps us understand the meaning of certain phrases, the importance of the geographical locations mentioned, etc. Through understanding the original message of the Biblical passage, modern hearers can understand what the author was trying to convey and apply it to their everyday lives. Furthermore, reading through the introduction of each biblical book will provide you with a good overview of the objective of the entire book.

Two study Bibles I can recommend are the HarperCollins Study Bible – New Revised Standard Version and the Life Application Study Bible – New Internal Version or New Living Translation.

I am convinced that the most underutilized and yet important parts of a good study Bible are the introductions to each biblical book. A careful reading of the introduction will help you see the big picture. Use study Bible introductions well, and you will be less likely to take a passage out of context.

Justin Taylor

2) Purchase a journal/notebook to write out your prayers or anything from your study that you may want to ask someone about later.

There will be some days that to read and pray will be hard. You may get distracted by other obligations and/or random thoughts. Sometimes, it's just hard to get out what you want to say. Write in your journal anything you need to talk with God about, anything you need to get off your chest; and most importantly, any impressions you get from the text.

3) Find a quiet place to read your Bible and journal.

Not only should you find a quiet place to read, reflect and journal. You may also want to take a few deep breaths to center yourself before you begin reading.

4) Pray before you read/study.

Jesus told the disciples that one of the primary responsibilities of the Holy Spirit is to guide us into truth (John 16:13). Before you begin to read, pray and ask the Holy Spirit to "quiet your mind, calm your spirit, give you understanding of what you are reading and speak to you through the text."

5) Instead of reading all over the place or going for speed, work your way through the Bible - 1 book at a time, 1 chapter or a few verses at a time, 1 day at a time.

This is to help retrain our mind from skimming when it comes to the biblical text. Also, you may not want to start with Leviticus, if you haven't spent time reading through a book of the Bible before. Given this brief devotional, you may want to go back and read the entire book of Joshua.

Perhaps you have never read or heard preached any stories of women in the Bible. Then the books of Ruth or Esther may be a good place to start. If you want to know about Jesus, pick one of the four Gospels – Matthew, Mark, Luke, John.

Again, don't worry about speed. You're going for quality, not quantity.

A good way to get a greater understanding from the text is to read the passage of scripture, more than once. Each time you read through emphasize a different word to see if that enhances the meaning for you. Finally, as we read sometimes it seems like words just "jump off the page."

When this happens, write the words down in your journal, later look them up in your Bible dictionary or concordance and think about what message the Holy Spirit is trying to convey to you by emphasizing this word.

6) As you read, ask yourselves the following questions:

   a) What is happening in the text?

   b) Who are the principle players?

   c) What can you understand about the verses you are reading considering the entire chapter and the purpose of the book, which can be found in the introduction section of each book of the Bible in most Study Bibles?

   d) What does this passage teach me about God?

   e) What does this teach me about how I am to live?

   f) How does it speak to what is currently going on in my life or in the world around me?

In addition, as you read, be mindful of whose perspective you are speaking from when asking these questions. For example, a reading of the story of the "Prodigal Son" can be read from the position of the Father, of the "prodigal" and/or of the "older brother."

Depending on your life situation you might want to ask yourself which perspective is more compatible with your current life situation and how God desires to speak to you through this Biblical passage.

7) Pray about what God has taught you about how you should think about God and how the Scriptures pertains to what is going on in your life, thanking God for revealing this through Scripture.

Sometimes the Word of God will bring comfort. Sometimes it will bring conviction, for example, showing you where you are out of alignment with the text. This doesn't have to bring about guilt. Simply tell God that you confess (agree with God that your behavior is out of alignment), apologize, and repent (ask God to help you live more in accordance with what you are reading.) Either way, ask the Holy Spirit to reveal to you what God is trying to communicate with you in the text.

8) Consider how you will "dwell" on what you have read each day.

Before you complete time reading and meditating on the Word of God, think about how you can/will reflect on this passage of Scripture throughout the day. For me, I sometimes make sticky notes and put verses on my bathroom mirror at home or over my desk at work to keep me mindful of God's promises and the verses that God is sharing with me.

When I get a chance to slow down, these sticky notes provide a prompt that invites me to ponder the lessons from my time of reading and study. They also serve as great encouragement in times of uncertainty and trouble.

Some friends I know put especially meaningful Scriptures on index cards so that they can keep them with them throughout the day and perhaps even memorize them using the index cards as flash cards. Whatever your preference, make a conscious effort to find a way to return to the verses you've read and to think about them.

You should also be looking for opportunities to apply the Scripture read for the day to what occurs during your day outside of your devotional time. For example, if you read a passage on loving your neighbor, think about how you can do this in helping others during the day.

9) Finally, consider making an investment to create a small library of reference tools you can use. Here's are some that you might want to start with:

- A Bible Dictionary explains the words, topics, customs and traditions, as well as provides insights into historical, geographical, cultural, significance;

- A Bible Exhaustive Concordance provides you with a list of all the verses which use a particular Biblical word, and which matches the version of the Bible you have purchased;

- A Topical Bible is like a concordance, but groups various verses by topic rather than word. This is helpful when the Biblical text deals with a particular topic without saying a word;

- A Bible Handbook, which follows the order of the books of the Bible and provides a quick reference of background notes, running commentary, maps and other important facts regarding the text; and

It seems odd, that certain men who talk so much of what the Holy Spirit reveals to themselves, should think so little of what he has revealed to others.

Charles Spurgeon

- A one or two volume Bible Commentary. Bible commentaries allow you to take advantage of the work of some of the world's best Biblical scholars by providing you with explanatory notes and their interpretations of the text. Commentaries should be consulted only after you have made a cursory study of the text.

I know that this can be intimidating and seems like a lot of work, but the promise far outweighs the cost as written in our key devotional text. Furthermore, consider how much money you spend on things that only return momentary value to you. You may discover that you are more than able to build a small library of Bible study tools. Also, many of these books are offered as used books through Amazon and through used book sites. I recommend Half Price books, www.bookbutler.com or www.thriftbooks.com for more economical purchases.

For those that are unable to make the investment in these Bible study tools, here are some helpful online resources:

- www.textweek.com – provides all sorts of information for lectionary texts. It provides online commentaries from historical and current scholars/pastors. To find some information about a particular portion of Scripture, click on the Scripture index, then click on the book of the Bible your passage is in. Next scroll down and look to the left to see if the portion of Scripture you wish to study is available. If it is then click on it to find more study resources

- www.biblestudytools.org – provides different types of the tools recommended above. To access study tools, click on the toolbar at the top where it says "study."

- www.biblehub.com – provides different types of the tools recommended above. You can click on various icons to access things like a concordance, Bible dictionary, and a topical Bible. Biblehub also allows you to show different versions of the Biblical text as well. For brave souls, it also provides tools to interpret the text in the original languages.

- www.theafricanamericanlectionary.com – provides worship resources, commentary and sermons from an African/African American perspective. Although it follows the Revised Common Lectionary, you can search for information on various Scriptures by entering in the Scripture verse or subject matter in the search box.

For those unfamiliar with the Revised Common Lectionary, here is an explanation of what a lectionary is and why churches used them from the Consultation on Common Texts:

WHAT IS A LECTIONARY?

A lectionary is a collection of readings or selections from the Scriptures, arranged and intended for proclamation during the worship of the people of God. Lectionaries were known and used in the fourth century, where major churches arranged the Scripture readings according to a schedule which follows the calendar of the church's year.

This practice of assigning particular readings to each Sunday and festival has continued through the history of the Christian Church.

WHY USE A LECTIONARY?

- A lectionary provides whole churches or denominations with a uniform and common pattern of biblical proclamation.

- A lectionary serves as a guide for clergy, preachers, church members, musicians, and Sunday school teachers that shows them which texts are to be read on a given Sunday.

- A lectionary provides a guide and resource for clergy from different local churches who wish to work and pray together as they share their resources and insights while preparing for their preaching.

- A lectionary serves as a resource for those who produce ecumenical preaching and worship resources, commentaries, Sunday school curricula, and other devotional materials.[16]

PRAYER STARTER:

Lord, I am a skimmer. I'm so used to looking at my phone for a text or a tweet – a sound bite of information that this is how I come to the reading and studying of your word. Transform my brain and my desires so that I might be one who "dwells in your

---

[16] Consultation on Common Text, "The Revised Common Lectionary," 2015, Accessed March 14 , 2018 . http://www.commontexts.org/rcl

word," while also navigating a world of sound bites. Thank you for the ways that my life is about to change as I spend more time in your presence and in the Bible. Amen.

JOURNAL QUESTIONS:

1) What is God saying to you through the Bible verse and the devotional?

2) How can you implement this step and move one step closer to your goal/resolution/promise?

3) What may hinder you in taking this step and how will you get around it?

4) How will you celebrate/acknowledge when you've taken this step (i.e., post on Facebook; share with a friend)?

5) If you didn't do this step, why or why not?

6) Identify what you need to address or resolve to accomplish this step, the support you may need, and when you'll begin addressing this.

CONCLUSION

Beloved, thank you for taking the time to work through this devotional on getting unstuck. I pray that as you implement the strategies outlined, you will find yourself a lot closer to your dreams and visions. I pray too that this little book will serve as a resource that you will return to any time you find yourself "stuck."

I know that as I have been writing, I have been challenged and encouraged by each of these steps. Also, as person who spends a lot of time scouring the web for research, and who has more books on my Kindle than I care to admit, I was particularly encouraged and challenged by the devotionals, quotations and research I found.

As I have shared with you the tools that help us be unstuck, I am the main beneficiary of their power. I have also been challenged to step up my game when it comes to reading, not skimming, and studying my Bible. It is easy to forget when you have read it several times before and make your living as theological scholar to just "abide" in the word of God. Because of this, I have changed back to a print Bible and a paperback notebook to journal my thoughts during my quiet time with God. It is easy to forget when you have read it several times before and make your living as a theological scholar to just "abide" in the word of God.

I am excited to implement these steps with you and to hear the testimonies of how God used this simple book to help you and me be "unstuck" and possess our promises.

Be Blessed.

Felicia

For more information or to schedule speaking engagements, workshops or group and individual coaching, please contact us at:

Felicia Howell LaBoy, MBA, M.Div., Ph.D.

The Orchestrated Effect, LLC

P.O. Box 114, Robbins, IL 60472

773 340-4306

felicia@drfelicialaboy.com

Follow me on Twitter, Instagram, Facebook and LinkedIn:

@drfelicialaboy

UNSTUCK

8 STEPS YOU CAN TAKE
RIGHT NOW TO POSSESS
YOUR PROMISE.

The Orchestrated® EFFECT

Integration into Harmony

www.ingramcontent.com/pod-product-compliance
Lightning Source LLC
LaVergne TN
LVHW021538080426
835509LV00019B/2704